Make it with

Rubbish

BOOK HOUSE

© Copyright for the English edition for the UK
and British Commonwealth by Book House

Original title: ¡Vamos a Crear! Recyclables
© Parramon Ediciones, S.A., 2001

Published in Great Britain in 2003 by
Book House, an imprint of
The Salariya Book Company Ltd
25 Marlborough Place, Brighton BN1 1UB

Visit the Salariya Book Company at
www.salariya.com
www.book-house.co.uk

ISBN 1 904194 98 2

A catalogue record for this book is available from the British Library.

Printed and bound in Spain.

Contents

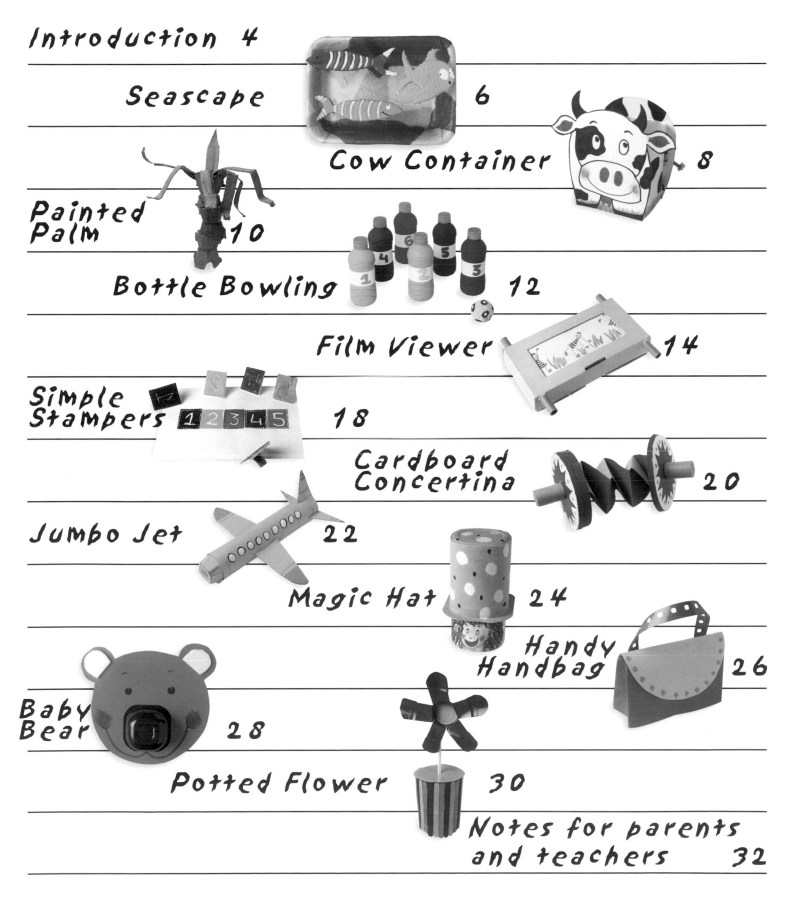

Introduction

Cardboard egg boxes and paper towel tubes; plastic cups, bottles and frozen food containers; milk and juice cartons, cans and polystyrene trays are all objects that people throw away every day. They are used to store food, to wrap presents, to protect fragile objects and so on. However, most of these throwaway materials can be reused in other ways. The process of reusing items is called recycling.

A lot of rubbish can be recycled to make fun crafts. How many times have you had to go out and buy cartons, boxes, wrapping paper, or other materials for your craft projects? Taking advantage of used supplies is a great way to develop your imagination as you give new shapes to objects that seemed to be useless. However, when you want to reuse items of rubbish, always make sure they are clean and undamaged.

This book will give you ideas for making original crafts. You can use a juice or milk carton to make a cow container for storing small objects; you can turn an egg box into a palm tree or a plastic dessert pot into the nose of a baby bear. Each of this book's twelve fun-to-make projects will help you see the many possibilities for recycling items of rubbish. You can complete these crafts following the easy, illustrated, step-by-step instructions. Better yet, after looking at the projects and the materials they use, you can invent your own craft projects.

To make almost any creation with recycled items you will also need some basic supplies, including scissors, sticky tape, glue, string, coloured pencils, paints and felt-tip pens. Watch for special instructions at the end of each project to try other great ideas. Sometimes making just one small change creates a very different result.

REMEMBER!
Whenever you see this symbol, or when you are using scissors, ask an adult to help you.

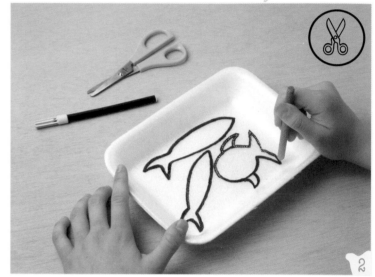

Seascape

You don't need an aquarium, or even a fishbowl, to surround yourself with sea life. This colourful scene is almost as good as the real thing.

1 Tear light and dark blue tissue paper into small pieces. Dilute white glue with water. Brush the diluted glue onto the pieces of tissue paper and press them onto a polystyrene tray.

2 On another tray, draw three fish with a black felt-tip pen. Trace over the lines with a bradawl then cut them out.

Toolbox

You will need:
- scissors
- white glue
- paintbrushes
- 2 polystyrene trays
- black felt-tip pen
- bradawl
- light blue and dark blue tissue paper
- different colours of paint
- cocktail sticks

3 Paint each of the fish a different colour and decorate each fish in a different style, such as stripes, spots or swirls.

6

4 Stick a cocktail stick into the back of each fish, in the centre.

5 Stick the fish onto the paper-covered tray wherever you want them to be.

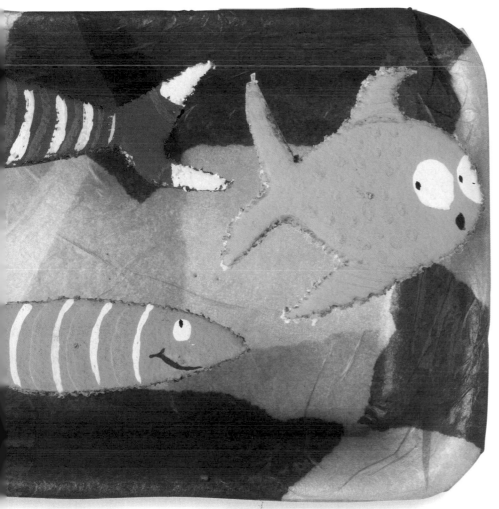

Move the fish around whenever you like – or make more fish so you can change your seascape!

Let your imagination soar

Other ideas:
Make just one large figure, such as an octopus, and stick it into the centre of the paper-covered tray.

7

Cow Container

When the juice is finished, turn the carton into this cute cow container.

Cow Container

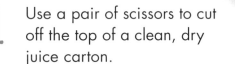

Toolbox

You will need:
- coloured pencils
- empty juice carton
- white cardboard
- black felt-tip pen
- scissors
- glue stick
- bradawl
- string

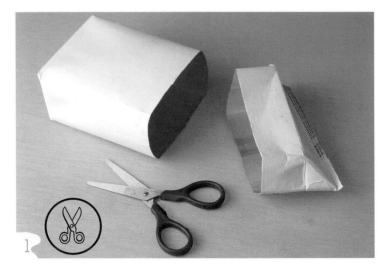

1 Use a pair of scissors to cut off the top of a clean, dry juice carton.

2 Cut a piece of white cardboard in half, across the width. On one half draw black spots with a black felt-tip pen and draw green grass across the bottom with a coloured pencil.

3 Wrap the drawing around the bottom of the carton and glue it on with a glue stick. Cut off any extra card.

4 On the other half of the white cardboard, draw the front and back of a cow and cut out the shapes.

8

5 Colour both parts of the cow with a black felt-tip pen and coloured pencils.

6 Glue the parts of the cow onto opposite sides of the covered carton.

Now put something special into your cow container.

7 Make a hole in the back of the cow with a bradawl. Thread a piece of string through the hole to make the cow's tail.

Let your imagination soar

Other ideas:
Draw a lion or an elephant or any other animal you like.

9

Painted Palm

Cut up an egg box and use the pieces to make a palm tree. Painting the palm makes it look lifelike.

Toolbox

You will need:
- scissors
- cardboard egg box with a flat top
- bradawl
- orange and green paints
- paintbrush
- thin, flexible wire

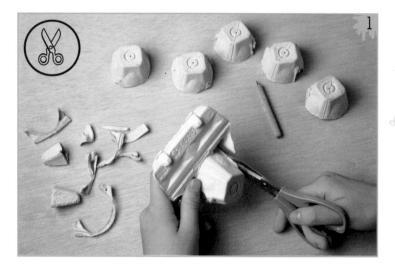

1 Cut off the cup-shaped parts of an egg box. Use a bradawl to poke a hole through the bottom of each cup, in the centre.

2 Paint each egg cup orange.

3 Cut a piece of thin wire and thread it through the holes in the painted cups, alternating one cup downwards, the next cup upwards.

4 Cut the top of the egg box into seven long strips. Make a hole with the bradawl at the end of each strip.

5 Paint the strips green to make leaves.

6 Stick the wire through the hole in each green leaf, then bend the end of the wire to hold the leaves tightly in place.

You have made a beautiful palm tree and you recycled a cardboard egg box that would otherwise have been thrown away.

Let your imagination soar

Other ideas:
Make two posts, each with three egg cups. Pin one end of a piece of netting material to the top of each post to make a clever hammock.

Bottle Bowling

A splash of paint recycles six plastic bottles into a colourful bowling game. Put numbered labels on the bottles so you can keep score.

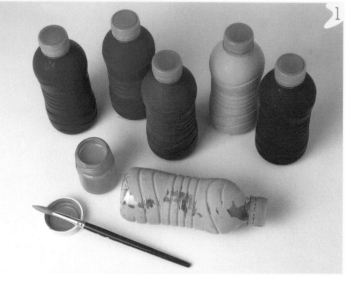

1 Paint each plastic bottle a different colour. Use bright colours, such as red, yellow, blue, orange, purple and green. Do not paint the bottle tops.

2 Cut six strips of white paper to make labels. Each strip should be long enough to fit around a bottle. Using coloured pencils, draw a large number, 1 to 6, on each label.

Toolbox

You will need:
• different coloured acrylic paint
• clear sticky tape
• 6 plastic bottles
• cardboard egg box
• coloured pencils
• white paper
• paintbrush
• scissors

3 Use sticky tape to attach a paper label to each bottle.

4 Soak the bottom half of a cardboard egg box in water until it softens.

5 Roll the wet box into a ball, squeezing it hard to remove as much water as possible so the ball holds together.

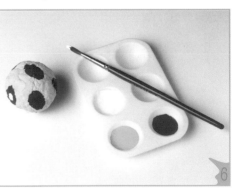

6 Once the ball is dry, paint it green and decorate it with red and white spots.

Let your imagination soar

Other ideas:
Use modelling clay to make the ball, or use any small ball instead of making one.

Put the bowling pins in position...
Roll the ball...Strike!

Film Viewer
Film Viewer
Film Viewer

Film Viewer

Show your homemade films on a homemade film viewer. Playing with a cardboard box has never been more fun!

Toolbox

You will need:
- paintbrush
- light green paint
- medium-sized, long, thin rectangular box
- black felt-tip pen
- clear sticky tape
- bradawl
- two thin cardboard tubes (like the tubes in a roll of fax paper)
- coloured pencils
- white paper
- ruler
- scissors

1 Paint the outside of a long, thin, rectangular box light green.

2 Using a black felt-tip pen and a ruler, draw a rectangle on one of the large sides of the box. Leave a wide border around the edge. Poke through the lines with a bradawl to cut out the centre piece.

3 At each end of the two long sides of the box, trace a small circle around the end of a thin cardboard tube.

14

4 Use a bradawl to punch out the circles, making holes for the cardboard tubes.

5 Slot a cardboard tube through the holes at each end of the box. The tubes should stick out on each side of the box (as shown).

6 Cut a piece of white paper in half (as shown). Stick the two pieces together at their short ends with sticky tape.

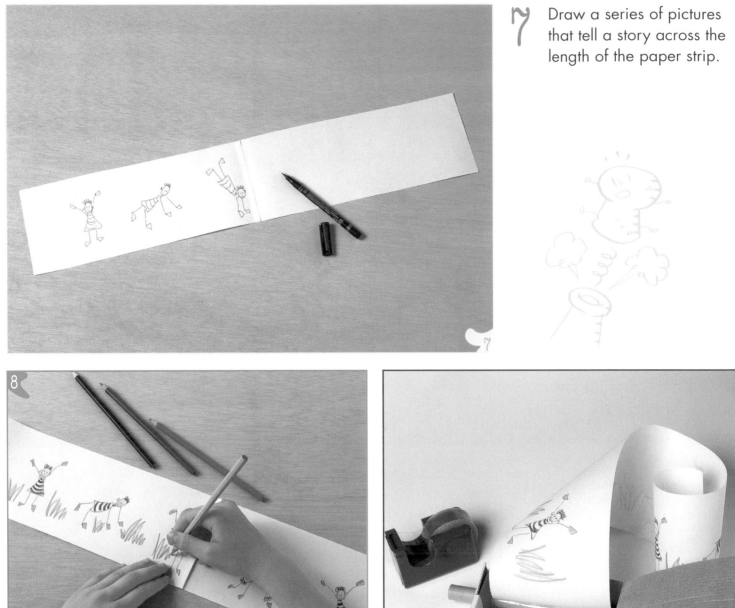

7 Draw a series of pictures that tell a story across the length of the paper strip.

8 Colour the drawings with coloured pencils.

9 Open the box and, on the inside of it, stick one end of the paper strip to one of the cardboard tubes with sticky tape. Make sure the pictures on the paper strip are facing downwards.

10 Turn the cardboard tube, rolling the paper strip onto it until you can tape the end of the strip to the other cardboard tube.

Lights. Camera. Action! Turn the cardboard tubes to show your film.

Let your imagination soar

Other ideas:
Make more paper strips with other stories on them so you can show different films.

Simple Stampers

Making your own number stamps is as easy as
1, 2, 3, 4, 5 – five simple steps to make five
simple stampers.

Simple Stampers

Toolbox

You will need:
- bradawl
- scissors
- polystyrene tray
- pencil
- glue stick
- 5 corks
- paintbrush
- different colours of paint
- white paper
- felt-tip pen

1 Cut out five square pieces from a polystyrene tray.
(Cutting the polystyrene is easier if you outline
the pieces with a bradawl first.) With a felt-tip
pen, draw a number on each square. Remember
to draw the numbers backwards so they will
be the right way round when you stamp them.

2 Press down hard with a
pencil as you trace over
each number to carve it out
more. Decorate the edges
of the squares by making
small holes with a bradawl.

3 Use a glue stick to stick
a cork to the back of each
piece of polystyrene.

18

4 Using a different colour for each stamp, brush a coat of paint around the number, covering the entire bottom surface of the square.

5 Stamp the numbers onto a piece of white paper.

Use your stamps on paper, wood or cardboard. What to stamp is up to you!

Let your imagination soar

Other ideas:
Draw flowers, boats, or whatever you like on your stamps instead of numbers.

Cardboard Concertina

A round cardboard container is just the right thing for making this colourful little concertina.

1 Paint both parts of a round cardboard container red, inside and out. When the paint is dry, paint a decorative border of white triangles and green spots on the outside of each part of the container.

2 Cut two strips of red paper, making them as wide as the inside of the container. With a glue stick, glue the short ends of the strips together. Repeat this step with strips of green paper.

Toolbox

You will need:
- red, white and green paints
- paintbrush
- round cardboard container
- scissors
- red and green paper
- ruler
- glue stick
- 2 corks
- clear glue

3 To fold the red and green strips together, place the end of one strip at a right angle to the other. Fold one strip on top of the other, over and over, to make a concertina.

4 Glue the ends of the concertina to the inside of each part of the container.

5 Paint two corks green.

Play your concertina by holding
each end by its cork handle
then opening and closing
the two parts of the container.

6 With clear glue, attach a cork to the centre of
each decorated part
of the container.
The corks are
the concertina's
handles.

Let your imagination soar

Other ideas:
Stand the closed concertina up on
one of its corks and give it
a spin. It becomes a
spinning top.

Jumbo Jet

You can use the cardboard tube from inside a roll of paper towels to make this jet.

Toolbox

You will need:
- black felt-tip
- cardboard
- scissors
- cardboard paper towel tube
- bradawl
- cardboard egg box
- yellow, green, white and black paints
- paintbrushes

1 Draw the wings and tail of an aeroplane on a piece of cardboard then cut them out.

2 Draw lines on a cardboard tube, marking where to cut slits in the tube for the wings and tail of the jet. Cut along the lines, first with a bradawl, then with scissors.

3 Slide the wings and the tail pieces into the correct slits on the tube.

4 Cut one cup off of a cardboard egg box.

5 Push the egg-box cup, open end first, into the front end of the cardboard tube so that most of the cup remains outside the tube.

6 Paint the whole plane yellow then add green decorations.

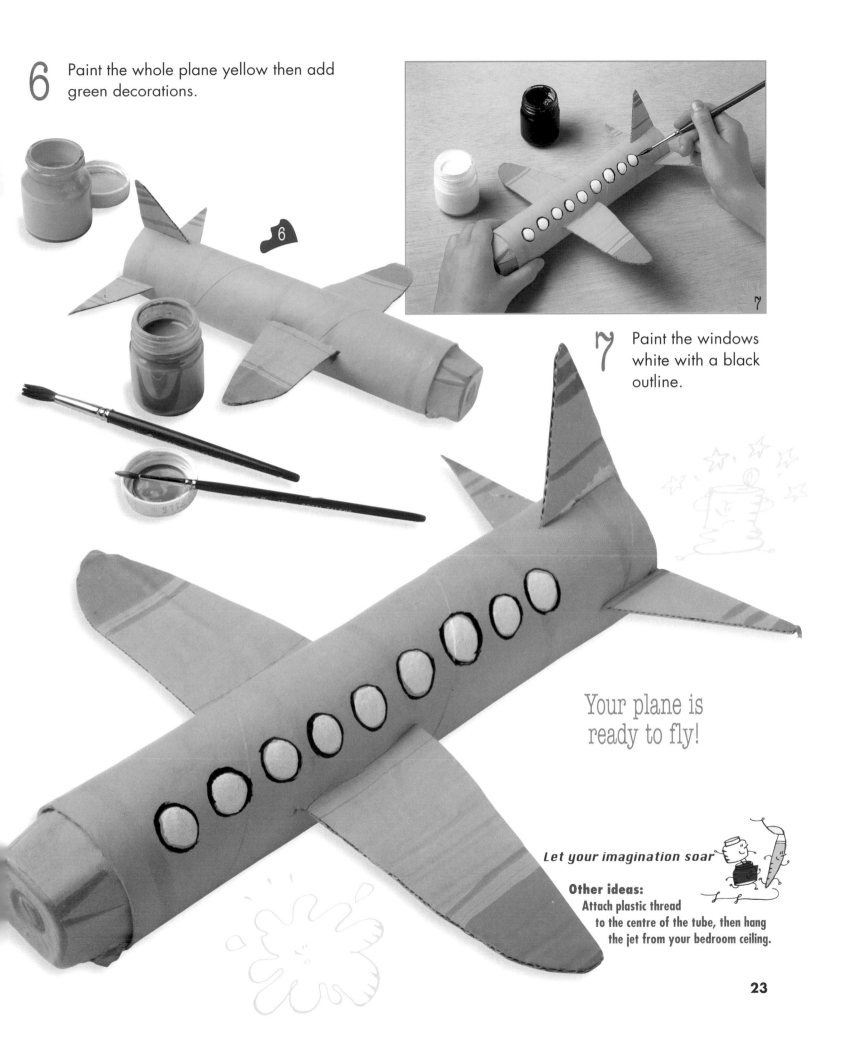

7 Paint the windows white with a black outline.

Your plane is ready to fly!

Let your imagination soar

Other ideas:
Attach plastic thread to the centre of the tube, then hang the jet from your bedroom ceiling.

Magic Hat

**How can two people wear one hat at the same time?
Make this magic hat to learn the secret.**

1 Paint a plastic yogurt pot green.

2 When the green paint is dry decorate the cup with spots of white and red paints.

Toolbox

You will need:
- glue stick
- paintbrush
- plastic yogurt pot
- white paper
- cardboard toilet tissue tube
- black felt-tip pen
- coloured pencils
- green, white and red acrylic paints

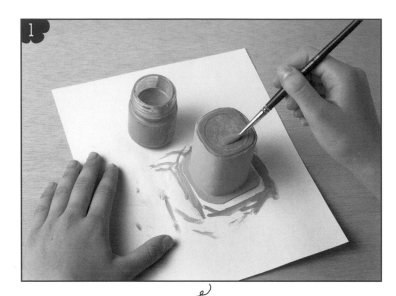

3 Cut a piece of white paper to a size just big enough to wrap around a toilet tissue tube. Before gluing the paper onto the tube, draw two faces on it. Draw one face directly above the other, with one face the right way up and the other upside down.

24

4 Wrap your drawing around the cardboard tube, using a glue stick to attach it.

5 Slide the yogurt pot over one end of the tube, covering one of the faces. The other face will look as if it is wearing a hat.

You can change the face wearing the hat – like magic! Just slide the hat over the opposite end of the tube.

Let your imagination soar

Other ideas:
Cover the yogurt pot with decorated paper instead of painting it. If you put a sock over your hand, you can use the magic hat as a puppet. The sock becomes the puppet's dress.

Handy Handbag
Handy Handbag Handy Handbag

Handy Handbag

Save your money in this bag *and* help the environment.

Toolbox

You will need:
- empty juice carton
- scissors
- purple paper
- glue stick
- yellow cardboard
- black felt-tip pen
- green paint
- paintbrush
- clear sticky tape
- green plastic file divider
- self-adhesive Velcro

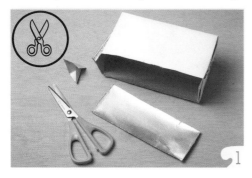

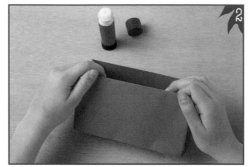

1 Cut off one of the long, thin sides of a juice carton.

2 Wrap a strip of purple paper around the carton. Use a glue stick to attach the paper to the carton.

3 Draw a semicircle on yellow cardboard and cut it out. The diameter (width) of the semicircle should match the length of the carton.

4 Paint green spots along the round edge of the yellow semicircle to decorate the flap.

5 Stick the flap to the back of the carton with sticky tape so that you can fold it over the open side of the carton.

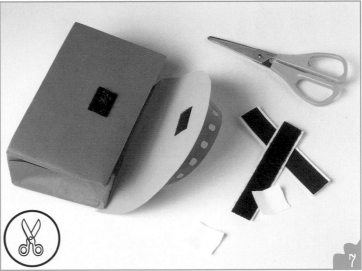

6 To make a handle for the handbag, cut the strip of holes off of a plastic file divider and attach the strip to the back of the handbag with sticky tape.

7 For a clasp, stick small pieces of self-adhesive Velcro to the front of the handbag and to the inside of the flap.

You'll be surprised at how much you can carry in your handy handbag.

Let your imagination soar

Other ideas:
Leave the handle off to make a clutch bag, or decorate the flap with whatever you like.

Baby Bear

An empty chocolate dessert pot is just the thing to make a cute little nose for this baby bear's face.

1 Draw the shape of a bear's face and ears on orange cardboard and cut it out.

2 With a black felt-tip pen and a red coloured pencil, draw on eyes, a mouth and cheeks.

Toolbox

You will need:
- scissors
- glue stick
- black felt-tip pen
- orange cardboard
- red coloured pencil
- polystyrene tray
- brown plastic dessert pot
- clear glue

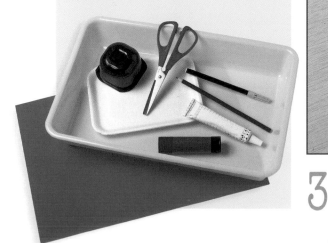

3 Draw two ears on a polystyrene tray and cut them out. Make these ears smaller than the ears on the bear's face.

4 Stick the polystyrene ears over the ears on the bear's face with a glue stick.

5 Trim off the corners of a dessert pot with scissors. With clear glue, stick the dessert pot upside down in the centre of the bear's face to make its nose.

With its nose in a dessert pot, what little bear wouldn't have a big smile on its face?

Let your imagination soar

Other ideas:
Use a different shape or colour of plastic container to make the nose of another animal, such as a pig.

Potted Flower

Watch how easily you can transform a plastic cup and a drinking straw into a decorative flower.

Potted Flower
Potted Flower
Potted Flower

Toolbox

You will need:
- scissors
- paintbrush
- yellow, red and green paints
- lolly sticks
- round plastic food container (such as an ice cream tub)
- clear glue
- red felt-tip pen
- yellow plastic file divider
- red plastic cup
- green paper
- clear sticky tape
- drinking straw

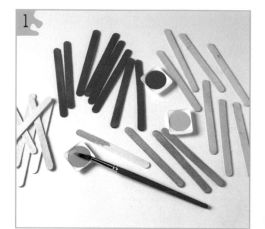

1 Gather enough lolly sticks to cover a plastic food container. Paint some of the sticks yellow, some red and some green.

2 Use clear glue to attach the painted sticks to the outside of the container. Alternate the three colours as you glue them on.

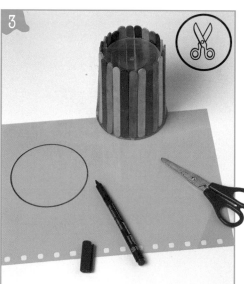

3 Use a red felt-tip pen to trace around the opening of the container on a yellow plastic file divider, then cut out the circle.

4 With the tip of some scissors, make a small slit in the centre of the circle. Glue the circle to the top of the container as if it were a cover.

5 Cut the sides of a red plastic cup into strips, trimming the ends to make them rounded. Fold the strips outwards one at a time.

30

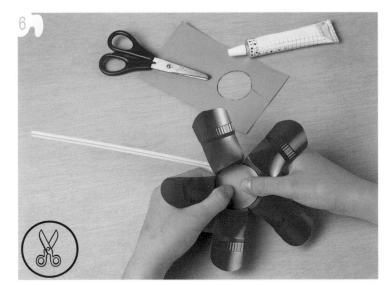

6 Cut a circle out of green paper and glue it to the bottom of the red cup to become the centre of the flower.

This flower is always in bloom and you never have to water it!

7 Stick a drinking straw to the back of the flower with sticky tape to make a stem.

8 Push the end of the straw through the slit in the cover of the flowerpot.

Let your imagination soar

Other ideas:
Cut several slits into the cover to make a toothbrush holder. Put marbles or stones into the container before you cover it to stop it from tipping over.

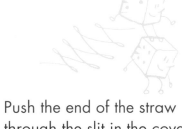

31

Make it with

Rubbish

Using recycled materials is a good method for developing a child's imagination. Everyday objects that are about to be thrown away can be used for lovely handicraft projects. It is a good idea to collect various sorts of materials and let children improvise with them.

Following are some suggestions for making each project, as well as a guide to the most appropriate age level of each one. It is important to point out that the suggested age is based on the degree of difficulty of the process, but the projects can be easily adapted to varying age levels.

p.6 **Seascape.** When working with younger children it is advisable to use thin sheets of polystyrene, which are easier to cut than trays.
Ages 5 and up

p.8 **Cow Container.** If you want to make the project easier, instead of covering the carton with paper it can be painted with black and white acrylic paints.
Ages 6 and up

p.10 **Painted Palm.** You can do without the wire and instead stick the pieces together with clear glue. A support can also be added in the shape of an island.
Ages 7 and up

p.12 **Bottle Bowling.** To make the bowling pins a little heavier, so they will stand up, they can be partially filled with gravel or sand.
Ages 5 and up

p.14 **Film Viewer.** If an adult helps to set up the 'film' around the cardboard tubes inside the box, this project is suitable for younger children.
Ages 7 and up

p.18 **Simple Stampers.** Following the same steps, but using fabric paints, the stamps can be used to print on T-shirts.
Ages 5 and up

p.20 **Cardboard Concertina.** This becomes a very simple project if the paper folded concertina-style is left out and the design is used as a spinning top.
Ages 6 and up

p.22 **Jumbo Jet.** If the 'cup' of the egg box does not fit well into the end of the tube, it can be stuck on with glue or sticky tape.
Ages 7 and up

p.24 **Magic Hat.** Before drawing the faces it is advisable to put the 'hat' on the tube and mark with a pencil where it comes down to.
Ages 5 and up

p.26 **Handy Handbag.** To make the bag even more realistic the carton can be covered with a piece of fabric, such as from an old item of clothing.
Ages 6 and up

p.28 **Baby Bear.** The support for the silhouette of the animal could also be a piece of cardboard or a sheet of polystyrene.
Ages 5 and up

p.30 **Potted Flower.** The project becomes much easier if, instead of sticking on lolly sticks, the container is painted with acrylic paint.
Ages 6 and up